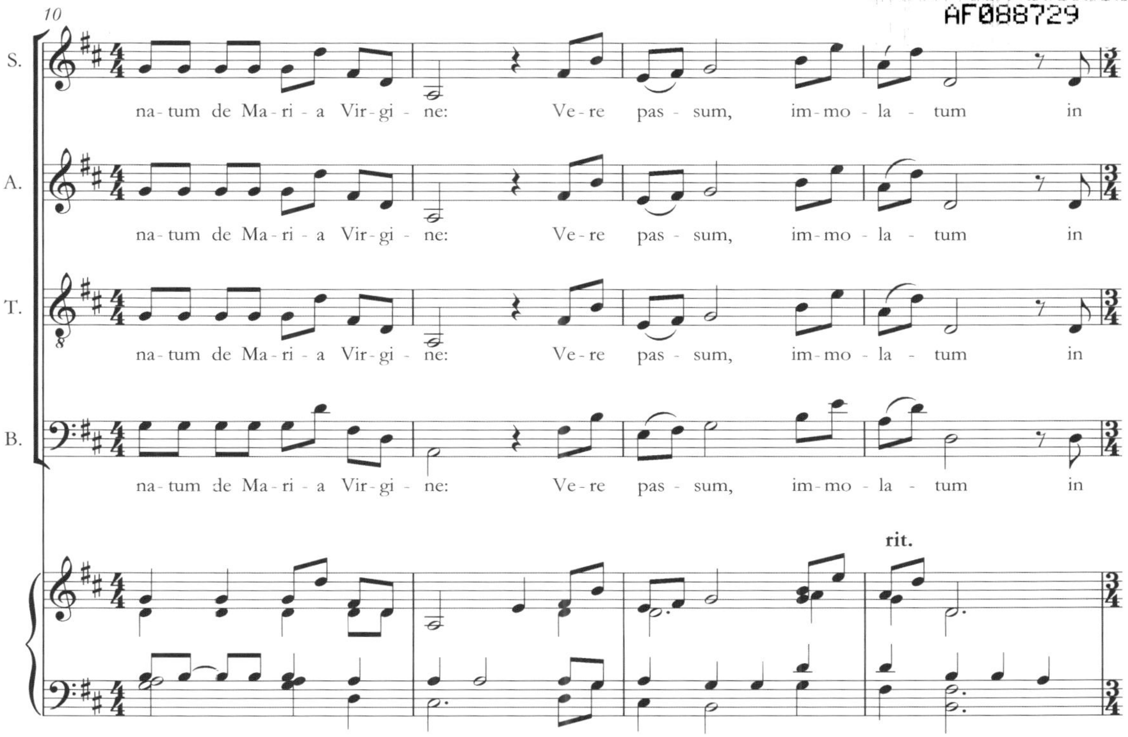
10
S.
na-tum de Ma-ri - a Vir-gi - ne: Ve-re pas - sum, im-mo - la - tum in
A.
na-tum de Ma-ri - a Vir-gi - ne: Ve-re pas - sum, im-mo - la - tum in
T.
na-tum de Ma-ri - a Vir-gi - ne: Ve-re pas - sum, im-mo - la - tum in
B.
na-tum de Ma-ri - a Vir-gi - ne: Ve-re pas - sum, im-mo - la - tum in
rit.

14
a tempo
rit.
S.
cru - ce pro ho - mi - ne, in cru - ce pro ho - mi -
A.
cru - ce pro ho - mi - ne, in cru - ce pro ho - mi -
T.
cru - ce pro ho - mi - ne, in cru - ce pro ho - mi -
B.
cru - ce pro ho - mi - ne, in cru - ce pro ho - mi -
a tempo
rit.

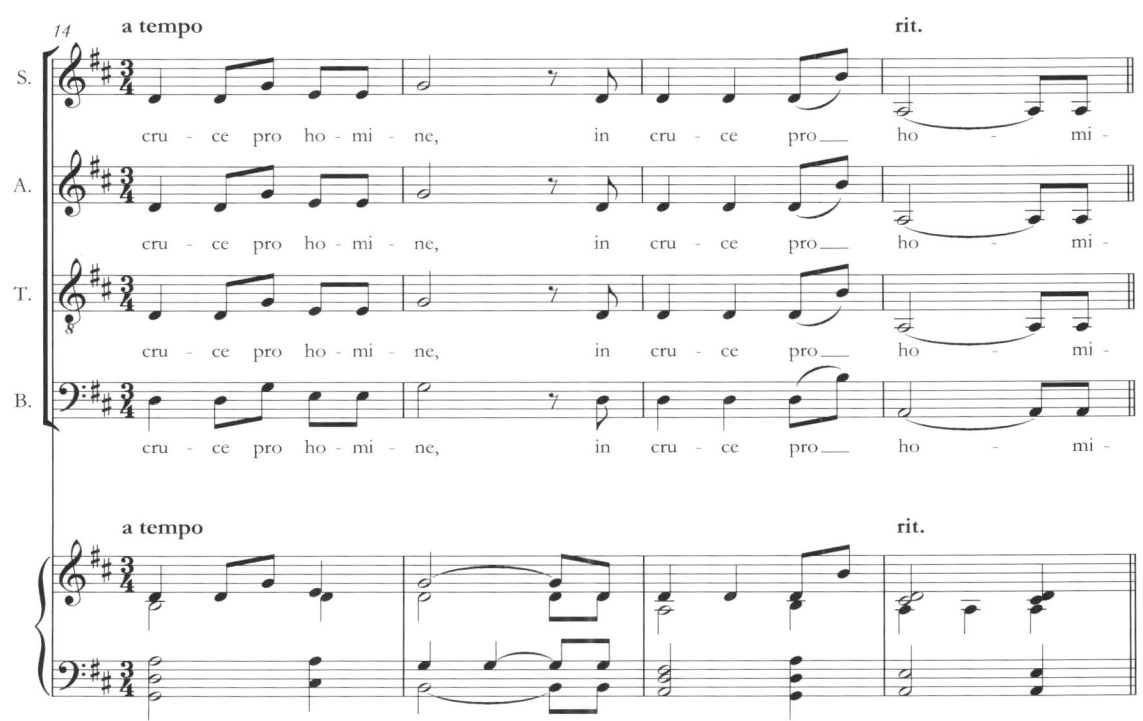

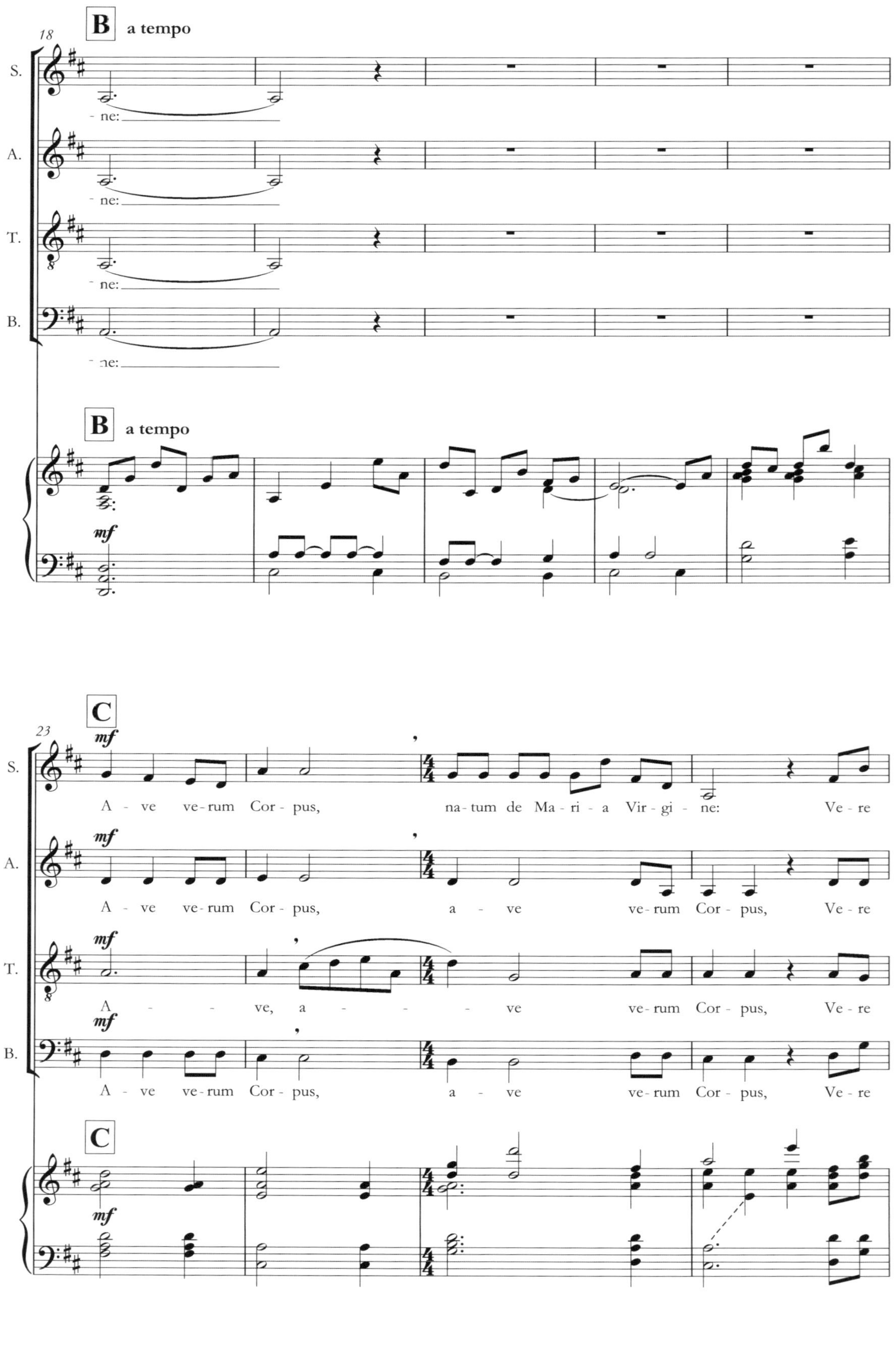
B a tempo
18
S.
- ne:
A.
- ne:
T.
- ne:
B.
- ne:
B a tempo
mf
C
23
mf
S.
A - ve ve-rum Cor - pus, na-tum de Ma-ri - a Vir-gi - ne: Ve-re
A.
A - ve ve-rum Cor - pus, a - ve ve-rum Cor - pus, Ve-re
T.
A - - - ve, a - - - - ve ve-rum Cor - pus, Ve-re
B.
A - ve ve-rum Cor - pus, a - ve ve-rum Cor - pus, Ve-re
C
mf

To the Wheaton College Conservatory of Music
Dr. Michael Wilder, Dean

Ave Verum Corpus

O Sacrum Convivium (Antiphon)

MORTEN LAURIDSEN

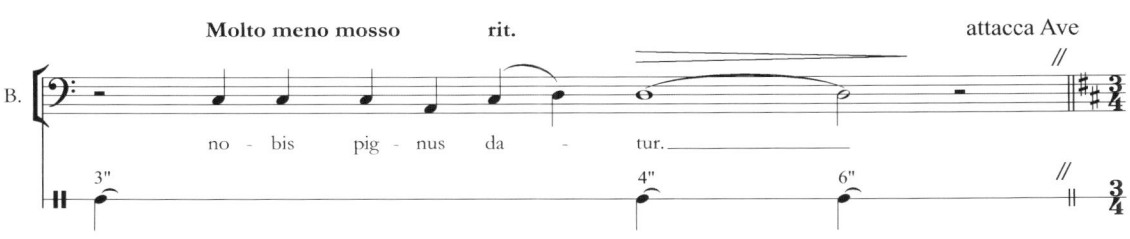

(duration of Antiphon: ca. 1'05")

© Copyright 2022 by Songs of Peer, Ltd. International Copyright Secured. All Rights Reserved.
This edition first published in 2023 by Faber Music Ltd as exclusive licencee in UK, Eire, Australia, New Zealand, Hong Kong, Singapore, Malaysia and South Africa. Brownlow Yard, 12 Roger Street, London WC1N 2JU

Ave Verum Corpus

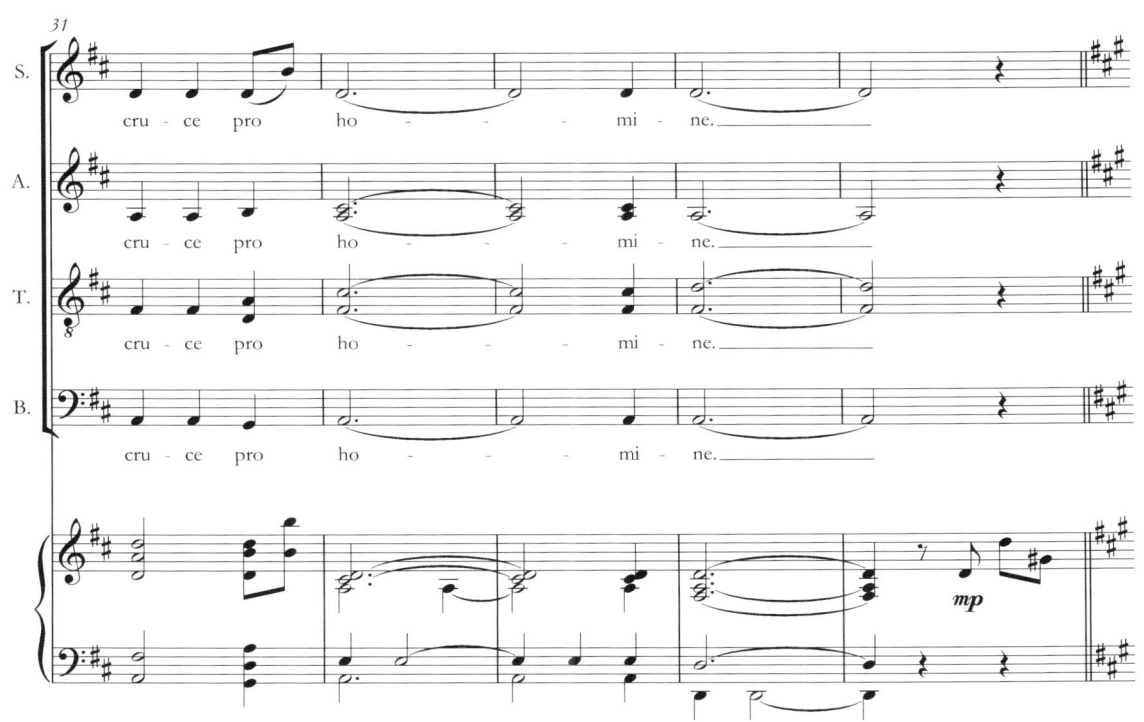

46
S.
A.
T.
B.
mf
Es - to
-ra - tum un - da flu - xit san - gui - ne:
-ra - tum un - da flu - xit san - gui - ne:

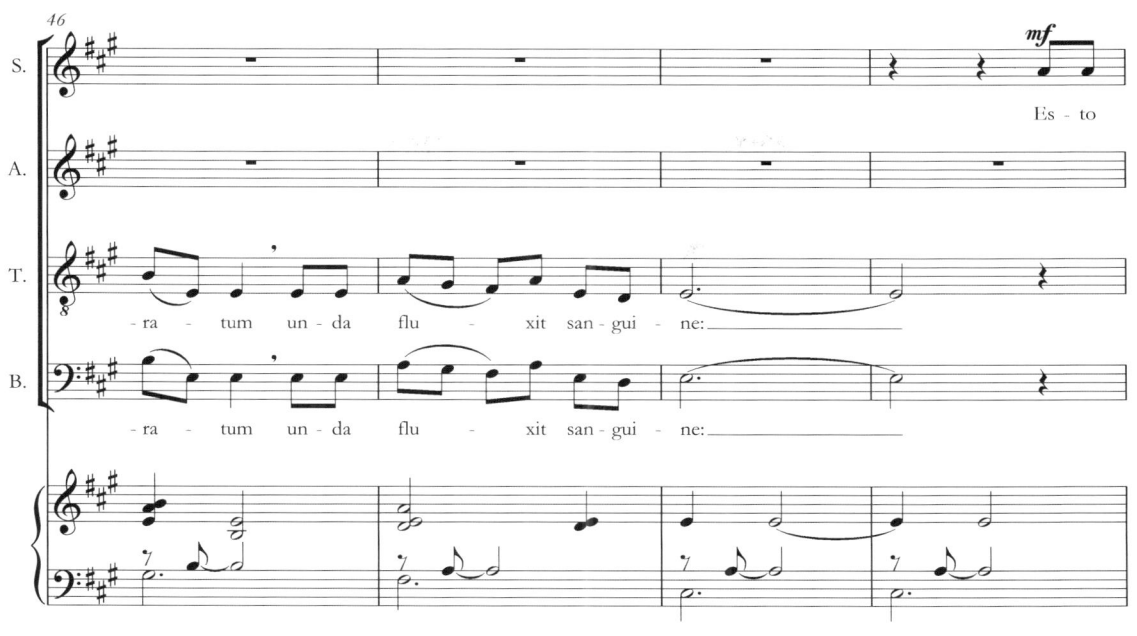

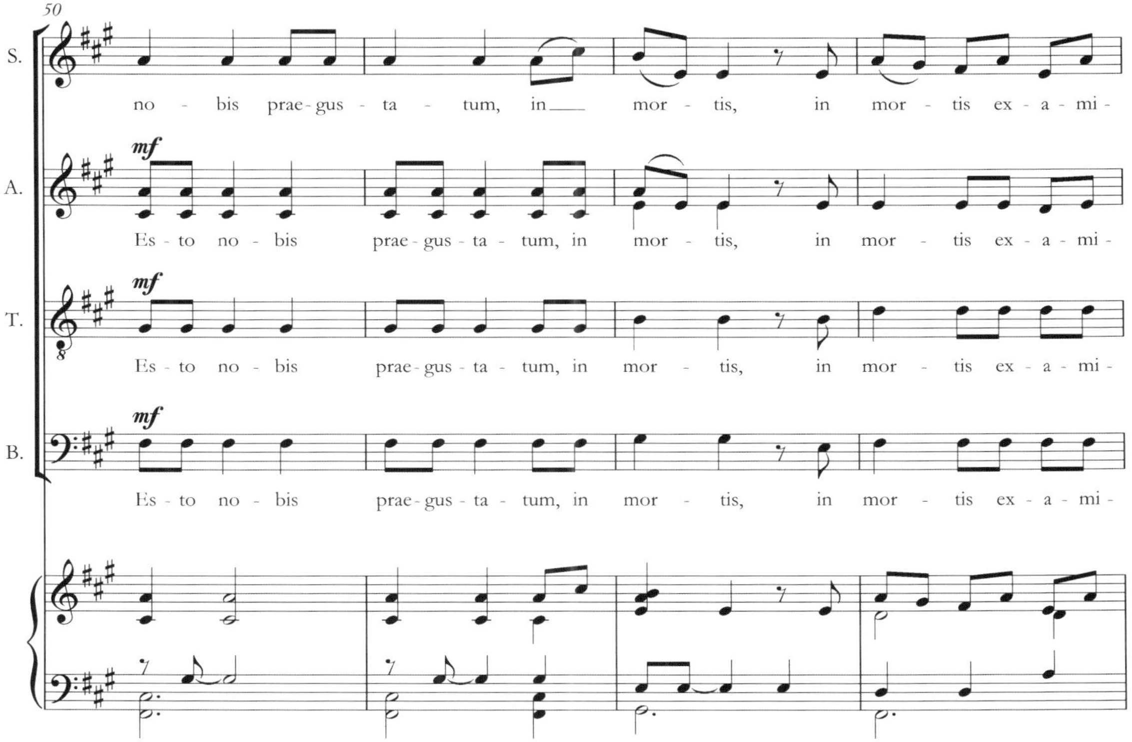
50
S.
A.
T.
B.
mf
no - bis prae - gus - ta - tum, in mor - tis, in mor - tis ex - a - mi -
Es - to no - bis prae - gus - ta - tum, in mor - tis, in mor - tis ex - a - mi -
Es - to no - bis prae - gus - ta - tum, in mor - tis, in mor - tis ex - a - mi -
Es - to no - bis prae - gus - ta - tum, in mor - tis, in mor - tis ex - a - mi -

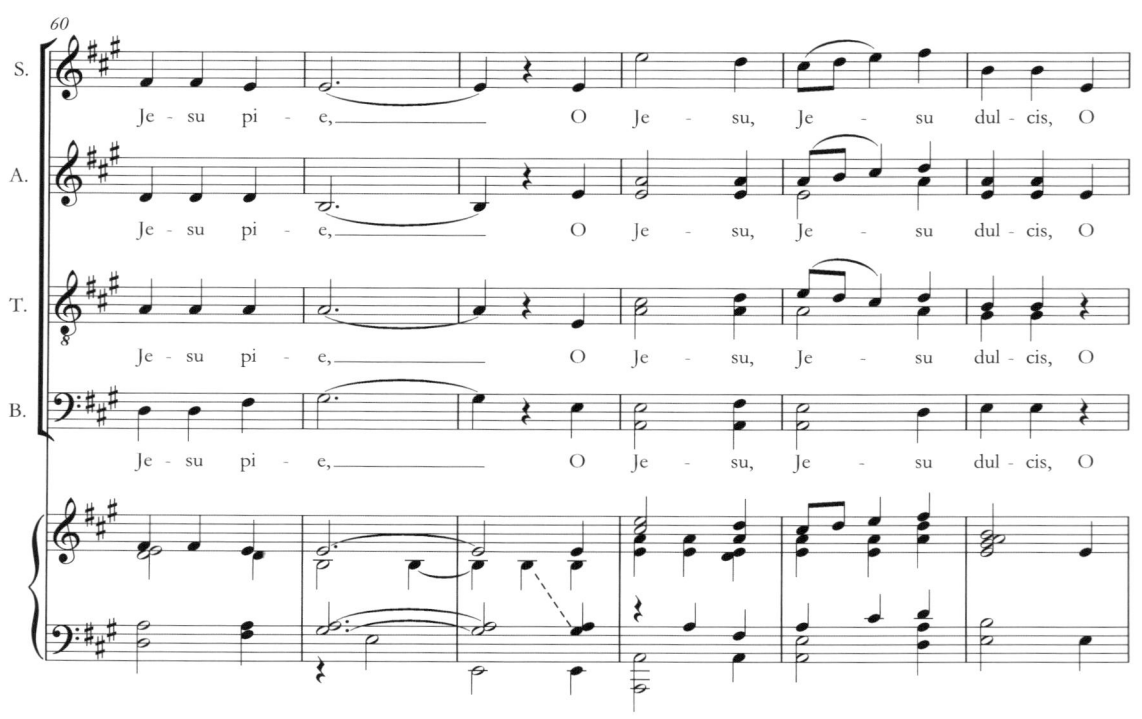

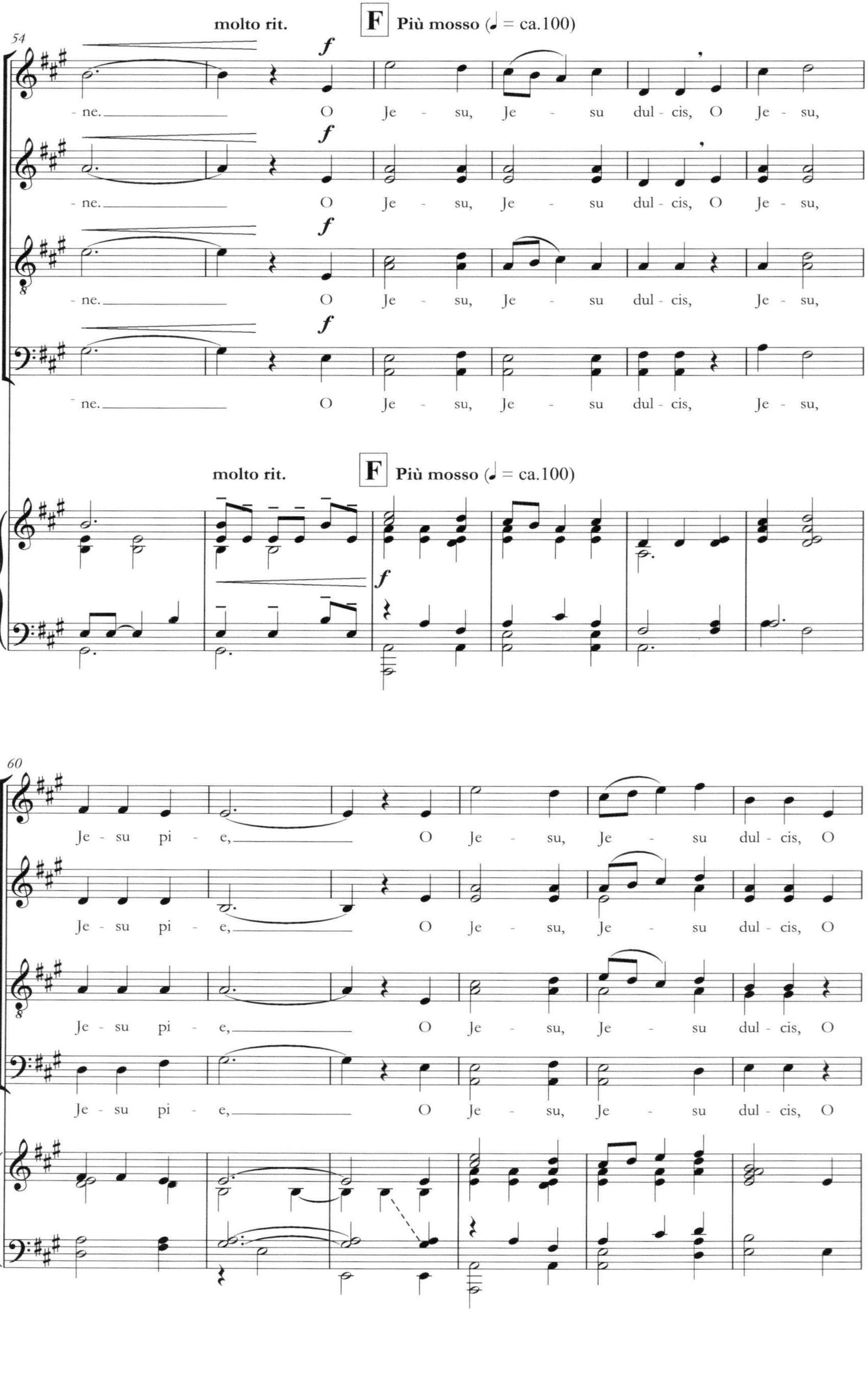
54
molto rit.
F
Più mosso (♩ = ca.100)
f
S.
A.
T.
B.
- ne. O Je - su, Je - su dul - cis, O Je - su,
- ne. O Je - su, Je - su dul - cis, O Je - su,
- ne. O Je - su, Je - su dul - cis, Je - su,
- ne. O Je - su, Je - su dul - cis, Je - su,
molto rit.
F
Più mosso (♩ = ca.100)
60
Je - su pi - e, O Je - su, Je - su dul - cis, O
Je - su pi - e, O Je - su, Je - su dul - cis, O
Je - su pi - e, O Je - su, Je - su dul - cis, O
Je - su pi - e, O Je - su, Je - su dul - cis, O

80
S.
A.
T.
B.
Je - - su Fi - li Ma - ri - - - - ae,
Je - - su Fi - li Ma - ri - - - - ae,
Je - - su Fi - li Ma - ri - - - - ae,
Je - - su Fi - li Ma - ri - - - - ae,

87
rit.
molto rit.
a tempo
mp
S.
A.
T.
B.
mi - se - re - re, mi - se -
mi - se - re - re, mi - se -
mi - se - re - re, mi - se -
mi - se - re - re, mi - se -
rit.
molto rit.
a tempo

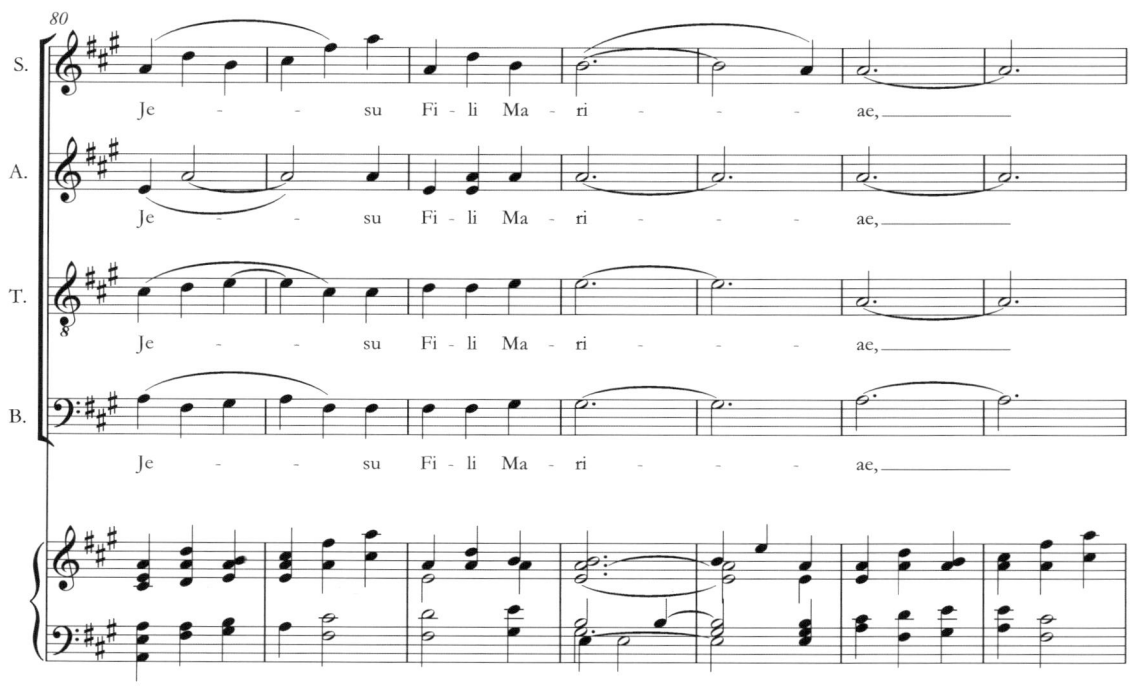

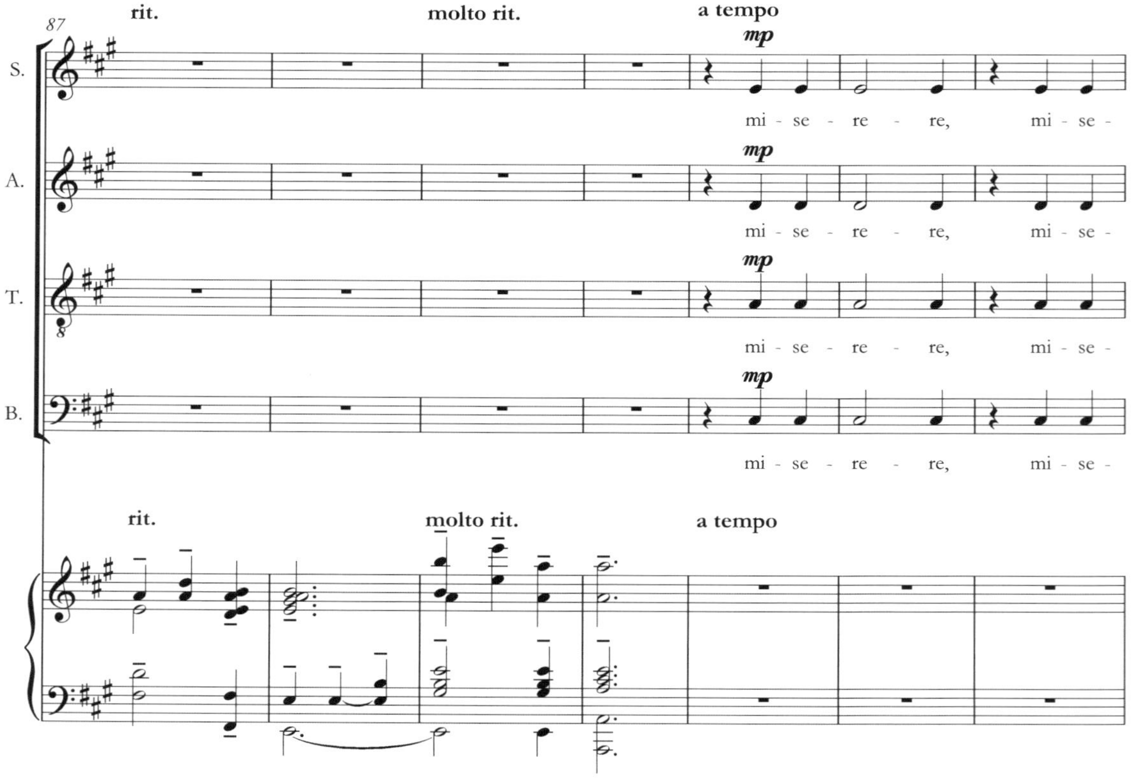

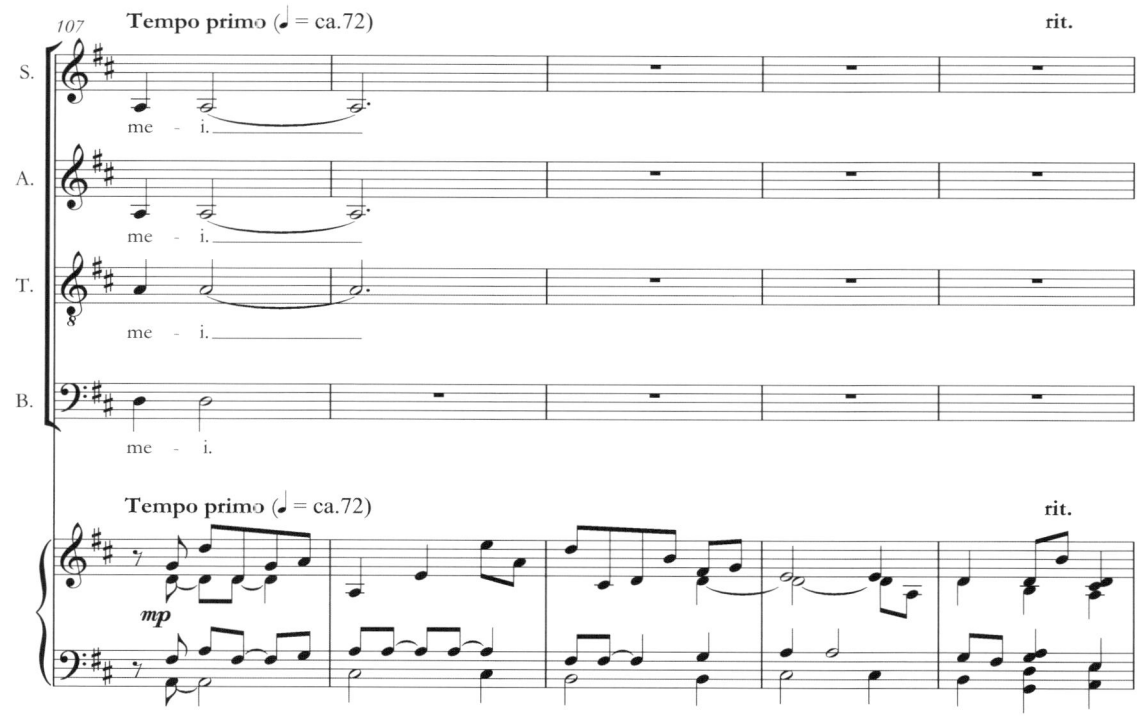

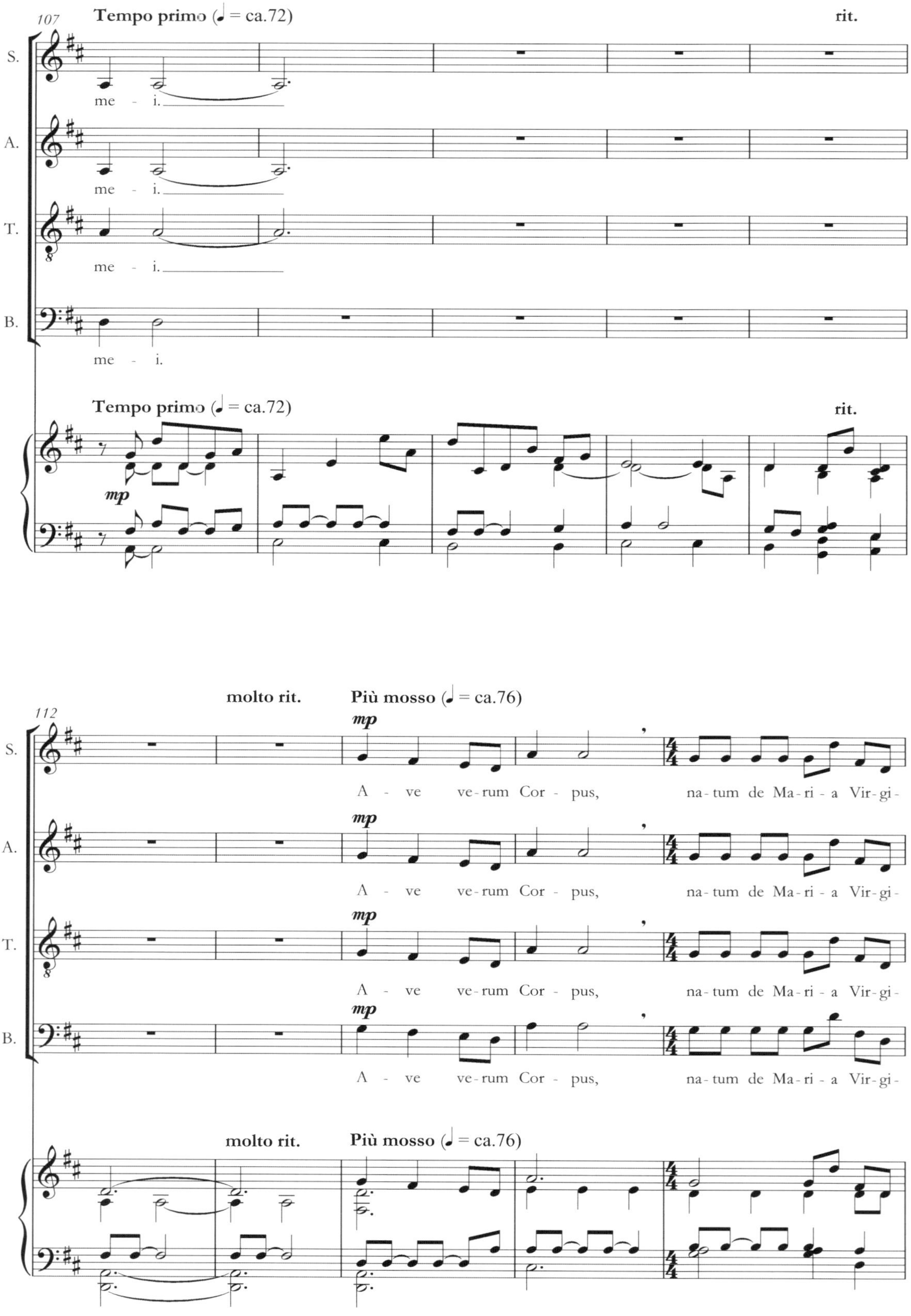
107
Tempo primo (♩ = ca.72)
rit.
S.
A.
T.
B.
me - i.
me - i.
me - i.
me - i.
Tempo primo (♩ = ca.72)
mp
rit.
112
molto rit.
Più mosso (♩ = ca.76)
mp
A - ve ve-rum Cor - pus, na-tum de Ma-ri - a Vir-gi-
A - ve ve-rum Cor - pus, na-tum de Ma-ri - a Vir-gi-
A - ve ve-rum Cor - pus, na-tum de Ma-ri - a Vir-gi-
A - ve ve-rum Cor - pus, na-tum de Ma-ri - a Vir-gi-
molto rit.
Più mosso (♩ = ca.76)

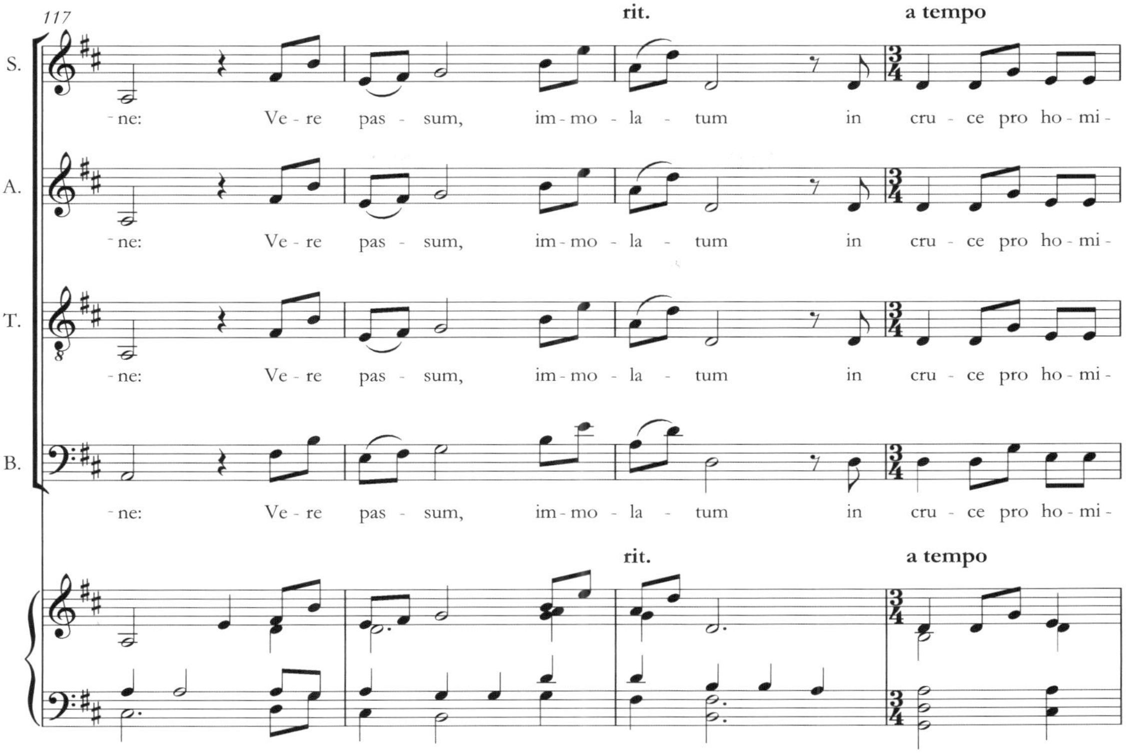
117
rit.
a tempo
S.
A.
T.
B.
-ne: Ve - re pas - sum, im - mo - la - tum in cru - ce pro ho - mi -
rit.
a tempo

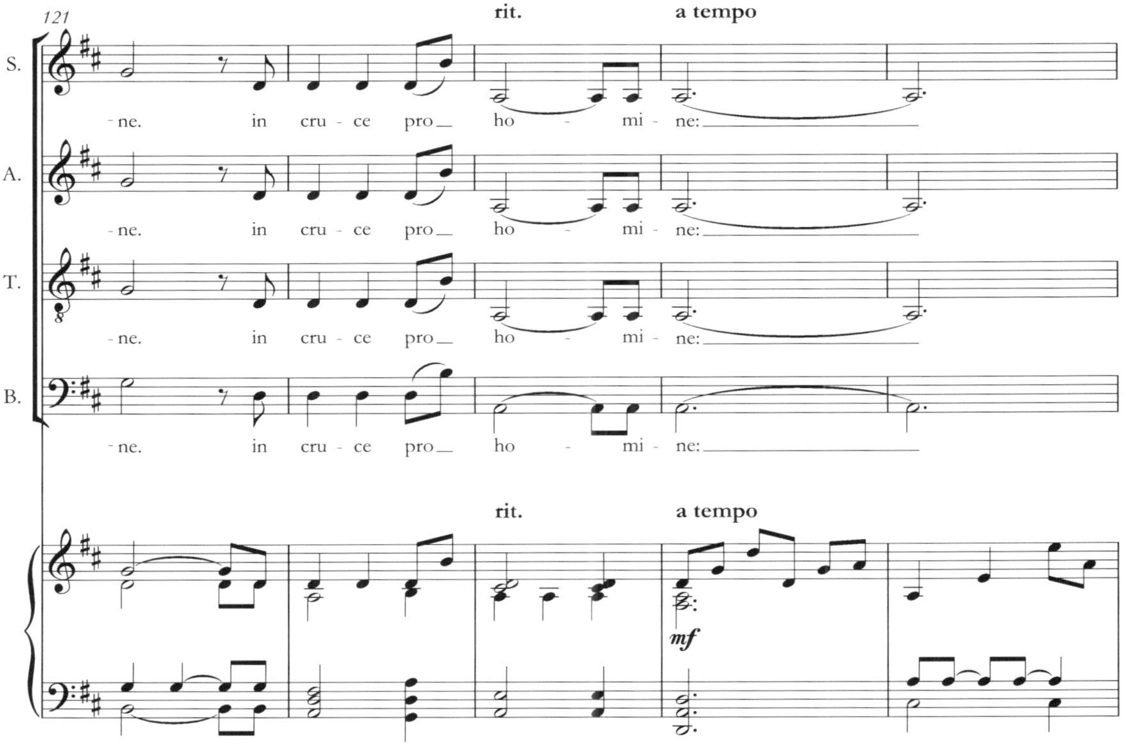
121
rit.
a tempo
S.
A.
T.
B.
-ne. in cru - ce pro ho - mi - ne:
rit.
a tempo
mf

134
S.
A.
T.
B.
-la - tum in cru - ce pro ho - mi - ne. in cru - ce pro

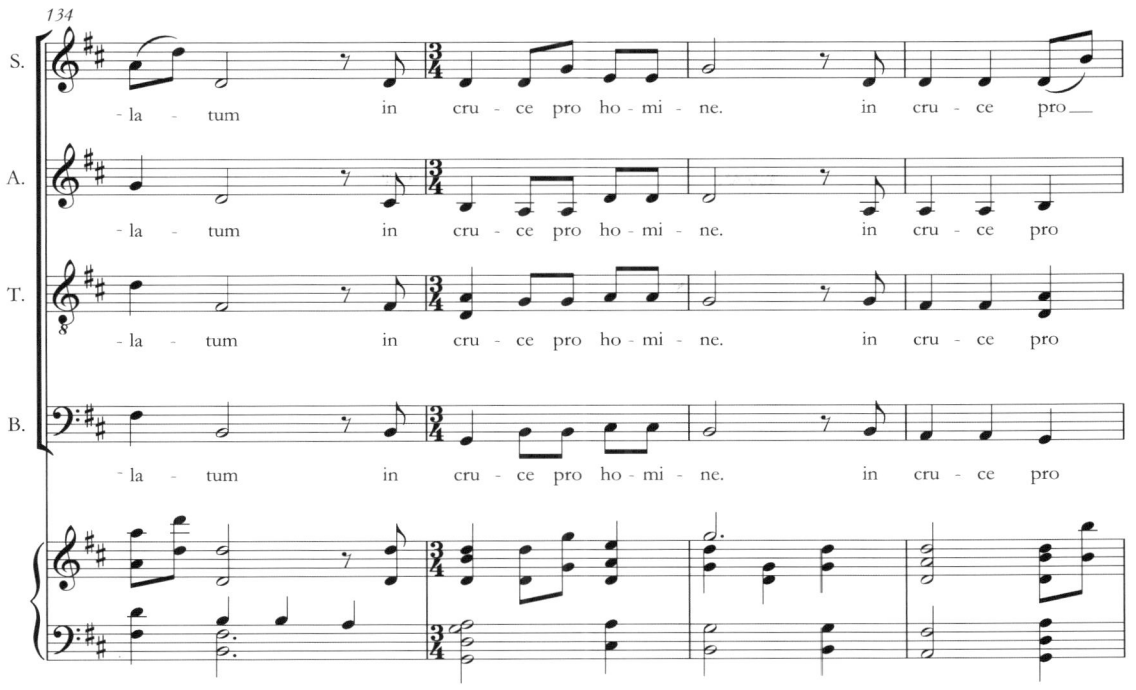

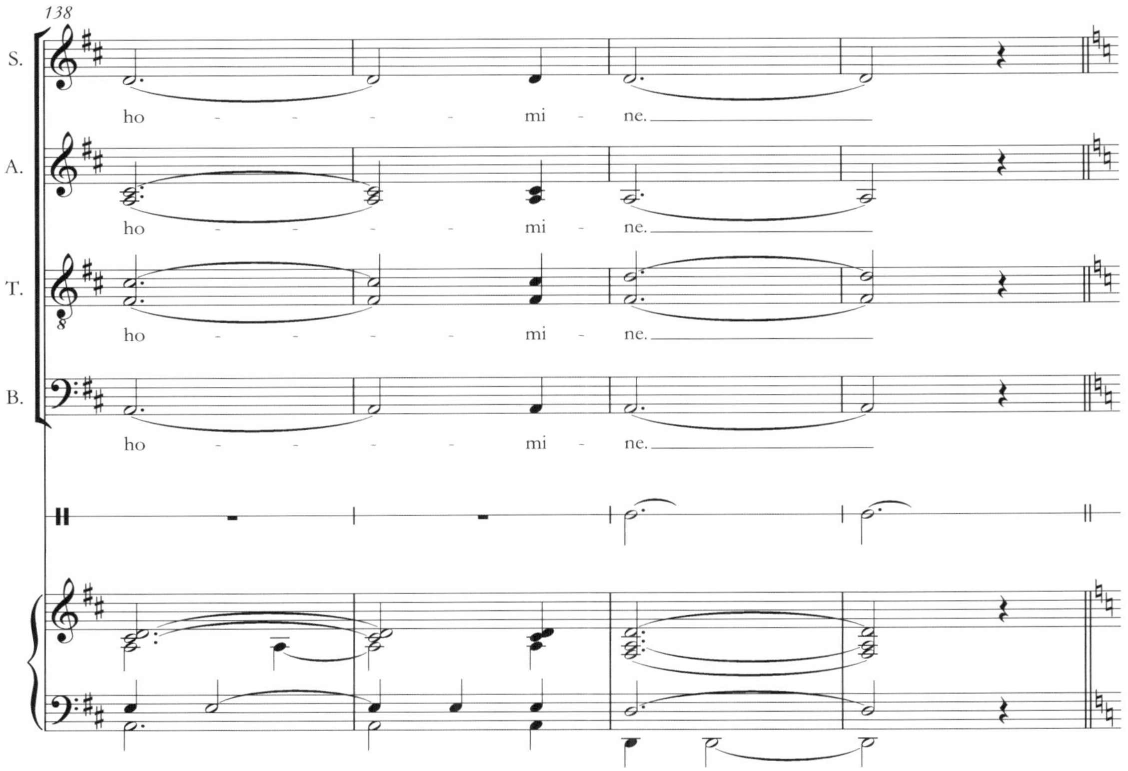
138
S.
A.
T.
B.
ho - - - - - mi - ne.

O Sacrum Convivium (Antiphon reprisa)

Alleluia

(Total duration: 10'30")

© Copyright 2022 by Songs of Peer, Ltd.
International Copyright Secured. All Rights Reserved.
This edition first published in 2023 by Faber Music Ltd as exclusive licencee
in UK, Eire, Australia, New Zealand, Hong Kong, Singapore, Malaysia and South Africa.
Brownlow Yard, 12 Roger Street, London WC1N 2JU
Printed in England by Caligraving Ltd
All rights reserved

ISBN10: 0-571-54285-9
EAN13: 978-0-571-54285-7

To buy Faber Music publications or to find out more about the full range of titles available
please contact your local music retailer or Faber Music sales enquiries:

Faber Music Limited, Burnt Mill, Elizabeth Way, Harlow, Essex, CM20 2HX, England
Tel: +44 (0)1279 82 89 82
fabermusic.com

CHORAL SIGNATURE SERIES

Difficulty Rating ★ ★ straightforward

WORKS INCLUDE:

Thomas Adès	The Fayrfax Carol
	January Writ
Julian Anderson	Four American Choruses
Jonathan Dove	Ecce Beatam Lucem
	Into Thy Hands
	Seek Him that Maketh the Seven Stars
	Wellcome, all Wonders in One Sight!
	Who Killed Cock Robin?
Vladimír Godár	Dormi, Jesu
	Regina Coeli
Howard Goodall	Jubilate Deo
	Lead, Kindly Light
	The Lord is My Shepherd
	Love Divine
	Promises of Grace
	Spared
	Sure of the sky, sure of the sun
	Veni, Sancte Spiritus
Adam Fergler	Agnus Dei
Francis Grier	Alleluia! I Bring You News of Great Joy
	Two Advent Responsories
Jonathan Harvey	Come, Holy Ghost
	Remember, O Lord
Malcolm Hayes	Corpus Christi
Nigel Hess	Jubilate Deo
Matthew Hindson	Home
Morten Lauridsen	Ave Dulcissima Maria
	Ave Maria
	O Magnum Mysterium
	O Nata Lux
	Ubi Caritas et Amor
Alexander L'Estrange	An Irish Blessing
	Epiphany Carol
	Hark! Mark the Music
	Hodie
	New College Service
	On Eagles' Wings
	Panis angelicus
	Prayers for Peace
	Song of the Angels
Wayne Marshall	Magnificat & Nunc Dimittis in C
Philip Moore	Lo! God is here!
Matthew Martin	Adam Lay Ybounden
	Behold, now praise the Lord
	Chester Missa Brevis
	Ecce Concipies
	Haec Dies
	Jubilate Deo
	O Rex Gentium
	Preces and Responses
	St John's College Service
	Ut Unum Sint
Colin Matthews	The Angels' Carol
David Matthews	Christ is Born of Maiden Fair
	To what God shall we chant
Nicholas Maw	One Foot in Eden Still, I Stand
Peter Sculthorpe	Lullaby
	Morning Song for the Christ Child
John Woolrich	Spring in Winter

The Choral Signature Series introduces a wealth of new or recently written choral music to choirs in search of fresh repertoire. The series draws in a rich diversity of contemporary composers and includes both lighter and more challenging works, offering a thrilling array of varied styles.

MORTEN LAURIDSEN
The music of Morten Lauridsen, Distinguished Professor Emeritus of Composition at the University of Southern California Thornton School of Music, occupies a permanent place in the vocal repertoire of the twenty-first century. His works include eight vocal cycles, art songs, instrumental works and a series of sacred motets, regularly performed and recorded throughout the world, many receiving Grammy nominations. Morten Lauridsen received the 2007 National Medal of Arts from the President of the United States 'for his composition of radiant choral works combining musical beauty, power, and spiritual depth that have thrilled audiences worldwide'. Lauridsen was the 2016 recipient of the ASCAP Foundation 'Life in Music' award.

ISBN10: 0-571-54285-9
EAN13: 978-0-571-54285-7

fabermusic.com

9 780571 542857